Christmas 2023

Dear Ru,
Never stop wondering,
never stop exploring.
There is so much for you
to discover.
All my love, Ior Tor

Ke Jing GOH · smeLyphan · Jessica Luu
Al Lau · Var Do... · ...Kung
Jacqueline Truong · Sus... Giang · ...en Li · Yen T...
Mandy Lee · Autumn Rose · SusSy... · Anh...onne Kw... · Xue...uang · Tingly · Luke Kang
Michelle Ngan Nguyen · A... Li · So... Me... · Au...Dochen · Perry · Christy Lau
Rebecca Castillo · Melanie Mao · MEIJI TOFU · Sarah Sasaki
James P. Crowley · Andy... · Jennet Liaw · Po Fung · Elvis Tran
Ying Ning · Ahmee Z · Helen Kim & Viet Nguyen · Kirstin · Shen Kaneko · Susan Tran
SW · Kendy Matassa · Benson Quach · Jessica Schleiger · Mai-Quyen Nguyen · Christy · Nancy Pan · Jennifer Kim · April-Park
Winson Quah · Clarisse Chen · Kade, Kira, & Rowan · Catherine Ng · David & Cally Wang
Mimi Cao · Asumi K · Regina Fang · Raymond Luu · Michelle Lee · Mochi & Mayu · Jane Tang
Donna · Tracy Liu · Catherine Woo · Tiffany Chan · Phillip Tran · Mielle · Karen Fine
Unera · Cynthia Zhou · Jack Chen · Christine Chen · Ethan & Rainie
Mariah Chammy · Rissa Choi · Mei · Adizz, Fgno, Lazer & JJ · Joseph, Yun, Julian & Max Ma
James Ng · Alex Malczynski · Shannon, Panu, and Troy · Lance Miyamoto · Mr & Mrs Helmut Ploog
Alice Wong · Garrett Wong · Puja Mistry · Zachary Park · Daniel M. Chung · Ro & Lana · Chao Family
Phillip Wang · Keemin, Holly, and Eleanor
Cindy Evans Nguyen · Renée Chan
Jing Shen CBIZ & Mayer Hoffman McCann PC · Victoria Chai · Seyla Mork · Jenny Le · Elizabeth Oh · Linda Phrasathane · Luke Tso
Alexander H. Yin · Katelyn Looi (and a few anonymous sprites)

MIMOCHAI

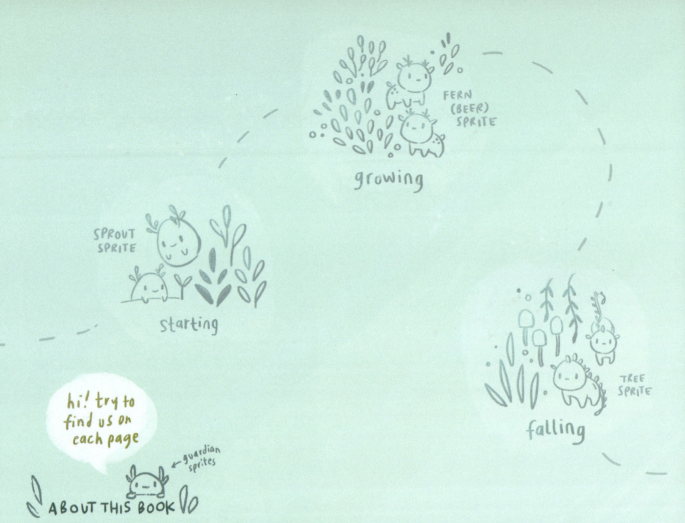

ABOUT THIS BOOK

This book was written, illustrated and designed by Mimi Chao. It was edited with the assistance of Julian Ma. The illustrations are hand-drawn and digitally colored. The font is Montserrat. The written text is hand-lettered.

Copyright © 2018 by Mimi Chao. All rights reserved.
First Edition 2018. Printed in China. 10 9 8 7 6 5 4 3 2 1

Library of Congress Cataloging-in-Publication Data: Chao, Mimi 1985— author, illustrator. Let's Go Explore. Summary: A pair of explorers travel through stages of adventure, experience and understanding to encourage explorers of all ages to discover their own journeys. Library of Congress Catalog Number 2018900051.
ISBN 978-0-9997794-0-8

Published by Mimochai Press, a division of Mimochai. 555 West 5th Street, Los Angeles, CA 90013
For usage rights and sales, contact hi@mimochai.com.

discovering — WING SPRITE

wondering — SKY SPRITE

dedicated to those finding their way

learning — CLOUD SPRITE

seeing — STAR SPRITE

up in a tree,

roll in the sea.

from way back when.

Pass through the clouds,

of some bigger thing.

play in
the shadows,

fly off a cliff.

Float by the stars,

let ourselves wonder

how it began.

wake up to see...

learn
to be
lost

Back at the start,

See with new eyes.

for the first time.

the ~~end~~ beginning

This is a story about taking on the adventure and exploring all our lives can be.

The same can be said about the story of how this book came to be. Mimochai was founded by Mimi Chao, who went on her own journey from being a corporate lawyer to finding her home in the world of storytelling and illustration.

Let's Go Explore was brought to life by our supporters, including (but not limited to!) the Early Explorers listed on the endpages of this book. We are so grateful for everyone who has played a part in this story.

thank you

The adventure continues.
Visit us at www.mimochai.com.

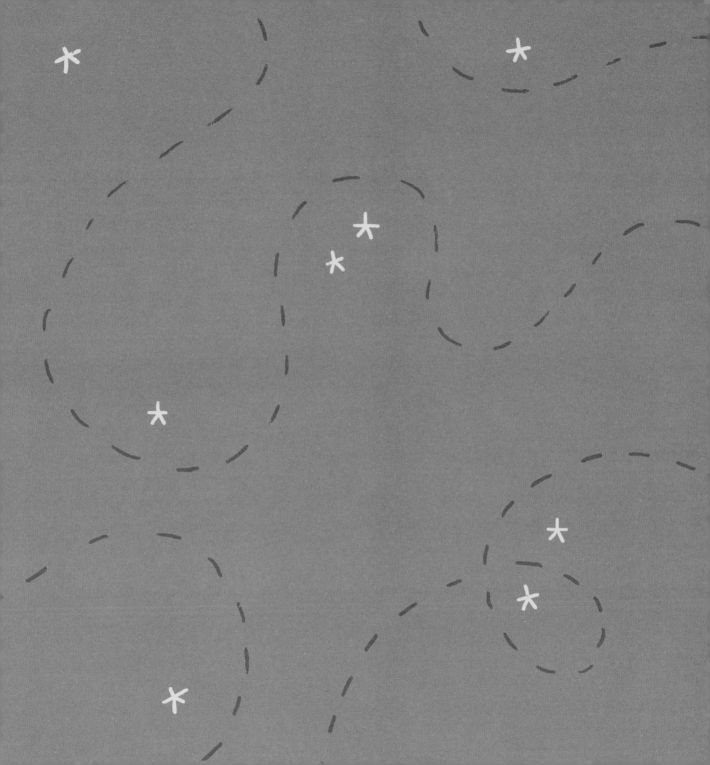

early explorers

GloriAnne . Rose F Dairo . Dan Cao . Huong Pham . Shefali Agrawal . Andrea Peng . Helen C. Joyee Li . Tiffany J Chen . Cynthia Zher
Alvin :) . Simon Le . Tiffany Lee and Kyle Ku . Jia-Mei Qian . Livvie T . Paul Bump . Raymond Tang . Lynda J. Lopez . Sandy L
Kelcie . Angelynn Jose . Keven Q . Lori Wong . Lilianne Gee . Ya Han Wu Fung . Steven
Chris & Patricia Shu . Terry Siu . Amy Noddings . Cecilia Ki . Pearl: R. Chan
Katherine Chin . David D Do . Michael D
Shaun & Candace . Taleeah Mesa
Linda Pan . Phuong & Nguyet . Phailrene Phanboonchan . Winnies & Meowsti
Randy Nguyen . Renee Joy Eguia . Jaimie M. Nguyen . Michelle Gonzales
Shelley Chen . Jillian Ma . Alexander Ngo . @infired_drawing
Evonne & Keaton Chia . Kimberley Wong . Kathy Vo . Jeram & Joyce Hyde . LiLing. T
Stephanie Bonit . Amber Nguyen . Rayce Yamasaki . Scott Sayasithsena . MN
Vanessa Tran . Joy Lai . Janice Chen . Jennifer Jou . Charles Wang . Seemei Ch
Geoff Stirling . Stephanie Hoang . Lily Estrada . Lime Yang . Picca . Michael Kaiser . Kelly Ngu
Joshua Hui . Christine Raymundo . Carmen T . Solene Kong . Jaimie Lim
Jessica Chao . Deany Bergmans . Ignacio Solano Oten . Maggie W
Kelly Fong and Clem Lai . Adrienna Chong . Finan Family . Kaling C . Sophie Lu
Ailee & Madeline Avis . Michael & Nicole . Vina Le . L.B. Autry . Karen M . Su Yin . Carolyn Chang
For Brandon & Katelyn . Joshua Miao . Jocelyne Chan . Jennifer Orr . Vivian Luu . Hooi Hooi . Kay Fung
Isa Tran . Vivian Kwan . Joan Ng Xin Ci . theINVprince . Brigette . Jessica Lui . Nancy Zhou . Carmen Chen
Daniel Won . Enoch Lau . Julian Ng . Jess Lin Park
anniegurumi . Samantha Guillen . Skylynn Mae Nakaji
Sammie Chan . Judaxil . Avery Xie . Junes . Lynn Kok